GRAPHITE

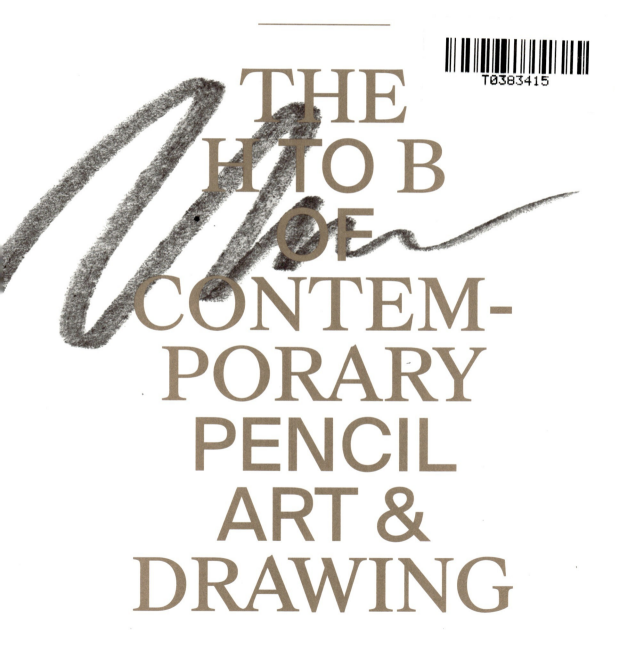

THE H TO B OF CONTEMPORARY PENCIL ART & DRAWING

First published and distributed by
viction:workshop ltd

viction:ary™

viction:workshop ltd
Unit C, 7/F, Seabright Plaza,
9-23 Shell Street,
North Point, Hong Kong
Url: www.victionary.com
Email: we@victionary.com

🅕 @victionworkshop
📷 @victionworkshop
Bē @victionary
🅟 @victionary

Edited and produced by viction:ary
Cover image by Misao Iwamoto
Creative direction by Victor Cheung
Book design by viction workshop ltd

ISBN 978-988-75665-2-6
Printed and bound in China

H ———————————— B

Graphite is a part of me, it's probably a part of you too. Elemental, strong under pressure and one of the oldest forms of inscription, graphite has lent itself to the hand-made mark of scientists, artists, cartographers, builders, draughtsmen and explorers. The truth is, we have been working with this medium our whole lives. A foundation for any artwork and most thoughts, graphite traverses the line made to mark a wall on a construction site whilst also being the medium we choose to delicately, painstakingly pour our imagination onto a piece of paper. Drafting ideas, mapping thoughts and erasing, there is the safety to change your mind. Graphite shapeshifts between strength and sensitivity, picking up the way you might have treated your page before drawing; collecting fingerprints on a surface long after it's been touched.

The monochrome medium provides a blank page on which to pour out our fantasies, juxtapositions and depictions of the world around us - examples of which can be seen by the great artists represented in this book. In years of scribbled and strong-toned conversations with graphite - in pushing it, exploring it, becoming more nuanced with the depth and textures — the medium begins to push back, revealing imperfections and indentations hidden in each surface. Fighting back, graphite offers up a remarkable resilience absorbed by anyone wielding the medium's considered strength.

It is my honour to introduce the works by the artists in this book, with whom I share a devotion hidden in shades of grey. Our most trusted tool, a conduit for creative thoughts, and a partner in this world with which to leave our mark. A sensitivity that becomes a powerful force to contend with, holding the history of an artwork and how it was created. We hope to learn from the steadfast resilience of our medium. Spending hours, days and months of hand-made marks, soaking the graphite back in, we leave silver fingerprints smudging Touch ID on silicone screens. Absorbed and drawn in, graphite is part of me and probably a part of you too.

Foreword by Jono Dry

Table of Contents   007

MARCUS JAMES

Born in 1973, Marcus James graduated from Central Saint Martins and received an MA from the Royal College of Art. He then worked on fashion collaborations with Alexander McQueen, Yves Saint Laurent, and more. In 2015, Marcus started his practise as a fine artist. His current work explores specific natural and cultural phenomena, and our relationship to the environment.

Marcus James

Bidean Nam Bian Summit
950 mm x 750 mm

009

GRAPHITE

Garnedd Ugain
950 mm x 750 mm

010

Marcus James

Beinn Fhada
950 mm x 750 mm

GRAPHITE

Meall Dearg
950 mm x 750 mm

012

GRAPHITE

Ben Nevis Summit
950 mm x 750 mm

014

Marcus James

Great End
950 mm x 750mm

015

GRAPHITE

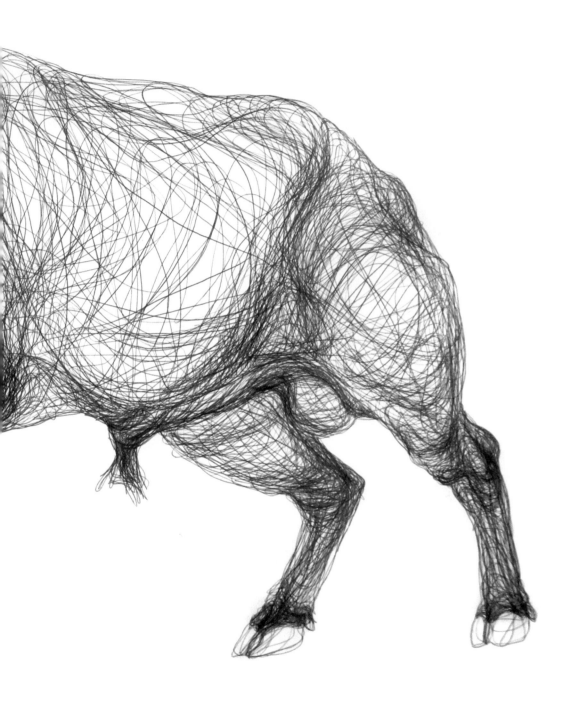

Marcus James

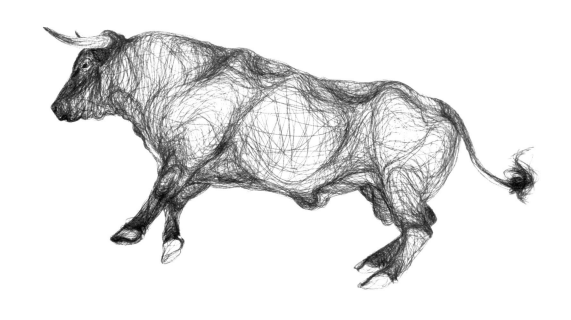

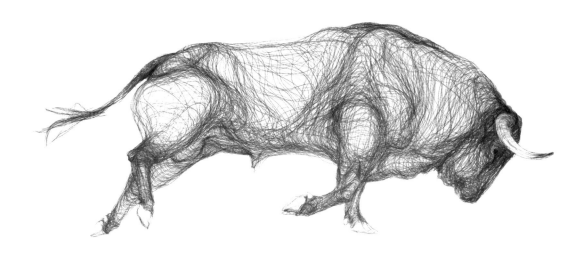

GRAPHITE

VENTERO
3500 mm x 1900 mm

CUMPLIDOR
3800 mm x 1700 mm

018

Marcus James

BOTERO
1800 mm x 2900 mm

019

JULIUS BUSH

As a self-taught product of Seattle, Julius extrapolates elements from personal experiences and existential inquiries. His works are influenced by cartoons, philosophy, biology, and human nature. While balancing interests of the heart and mind, this intention of displaying feelings and thoughts results in the materialisation of intangibles into a palpable thought, presented to resonate as a moment.

Julius Bush

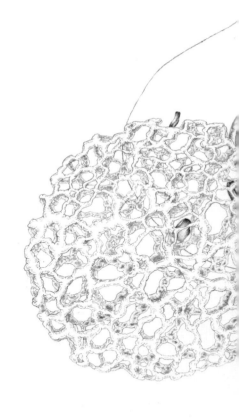

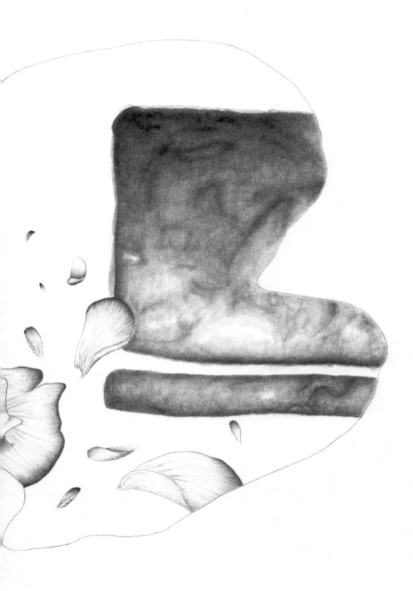

Julius Bush

The Wind Used To Speak
558.8 mm x 762 mm

GRAPHITE

The Moon Poured Honey Light
558.8 mm x 762 mm

Julius Bush

Polarize
558.8 mm x 762 mm

ERIKA SHIBA

Erika Shiba is a Japanese printmaker and drawer born and raised in Hong Kong. She received her BFA in 2018 from Parsons School of Design for Illustration and Printmaking, and received her MFA in Printmaking at Illinois State University in 2021. She has been included in group shows at Blanc Gallery, Feinkunst Krüger and the International Print Centre of New York.

Erika Shiba

Herethere
305 mm x 381 mm

Erika Shiba

Untitled
279 mm x 356 mm

029

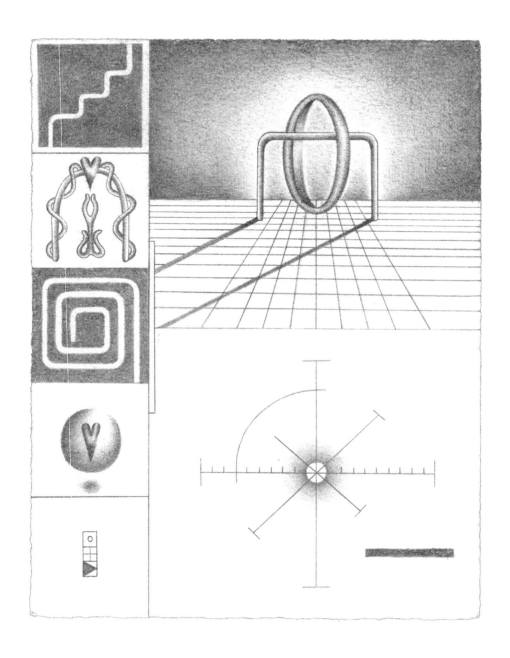

GRAPHITE

Study of Mentalscape
252 mm x 203 mm

030

Erika Shiba

{2022/2001}
178 mm x 254 mm

031

GILLES MAZZUFFERI

Gilles Mazzufferi is a photographer and plastic artist based in France. After training in photography, he also studied music at a conservatory. Since 2015, he draws mainly in graphite, charcoal and pastels. For several years, Gilles has focused on the theme of collective unconsciousness, which takes the form of an imaginary world of forests within our psyche.

Gilles Mazzufferi

Meteors
900 mm x 750 mm

033

Modern Myth
900 mm x 750 mm

Gilles Mazzufferi

Between Two
900 mm x 750 mm

035

GRAPHITE

Artemis
900 mm x 750 mm

036

Gilles Mazzufferi

The Circle
900 mm x 750 mm

Gilles Mazzufferi

L'invention de la morale
2000 mm x 2300 mm

GRAPHITE

Abandonment
750 mm x 900 mm

040

Gilles Mazzufferi

NIELS JANSSEN

Niels Janssen received his education at the Royal Academy of Art in the Hague, where he settled after graduation. He spends most of his time working in his studio and recently initiated a new project, attracting supporters for his independent work. He has also been active as an art teacher for nearly 25 years.

Niels Janssen

The Big Bang Prophecy
1220 mm x 930 mm

043

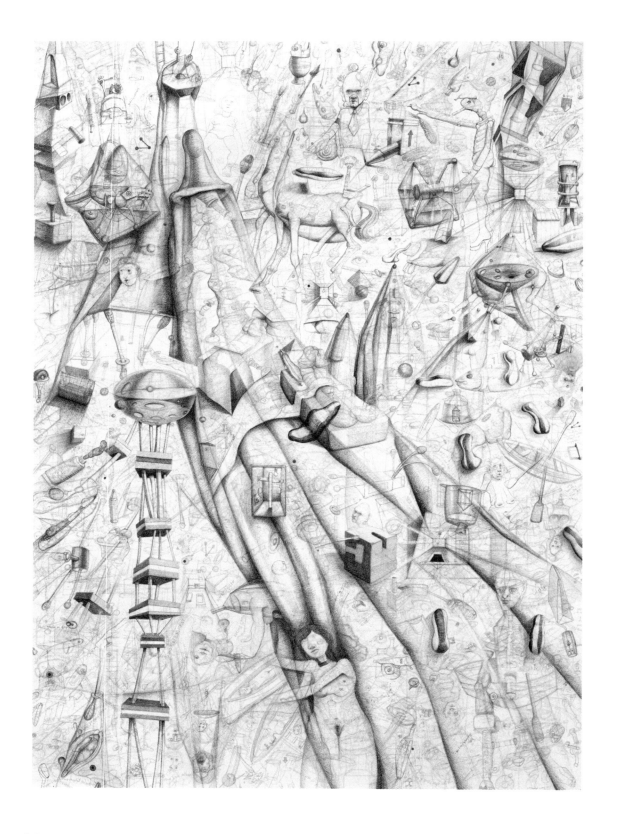

GRAPHITE

Psychograph 2
1400 mm x 1000 mm

044

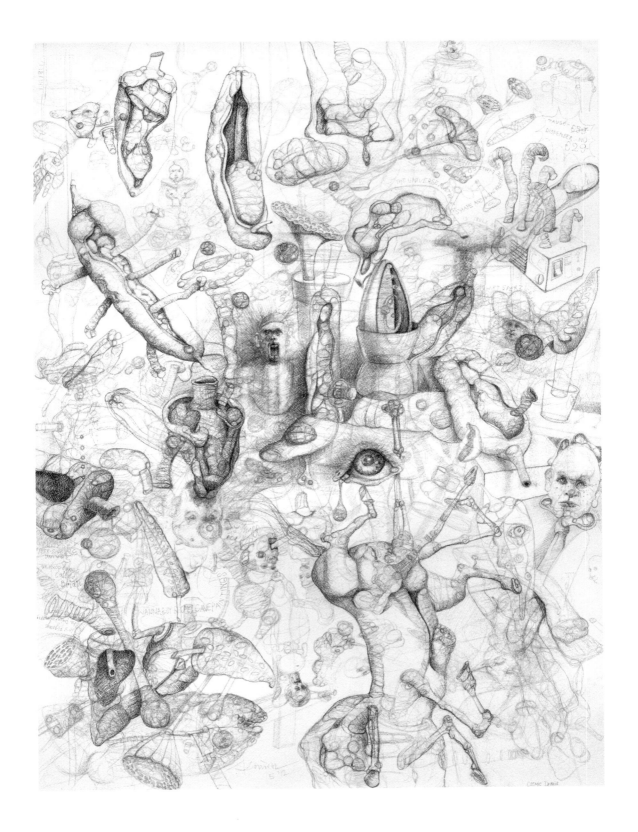

Niels Janssen

Cosmic Debris
765 mm x 565 mm

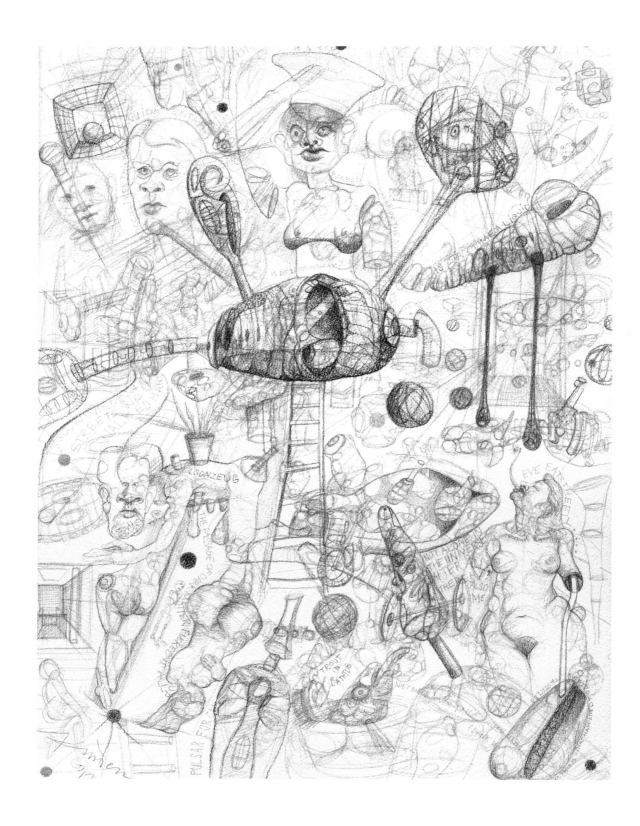

GRAPHITE

Agitarius
370 mm x 270 mm

046

Niels Janssen

Travellers
2000 mm x 1800 mm

047

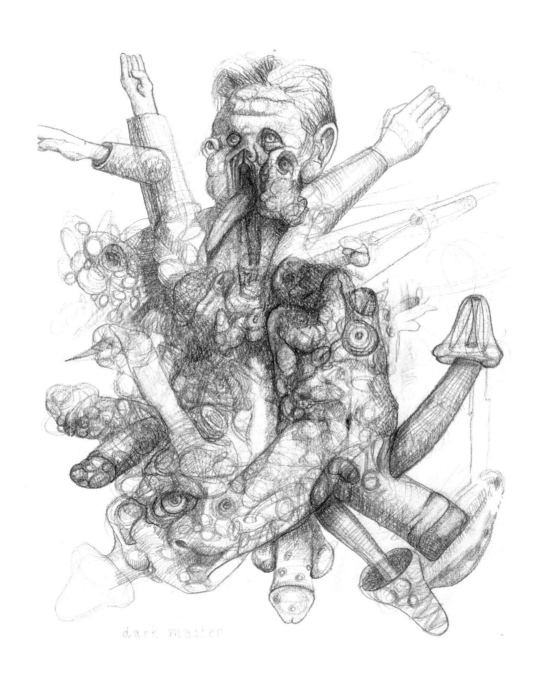

dark matter

GRAPHITE

Dark Matter
200 mm x 155 mm

048

Niels Janssen

Labyrinth
295 mm x 205 mm

CANDAN İŞCAN

Candan İşcan received her BA and MFA from İ.D.Bilkent University and moved to Istanbul in 2013, where she worked as an art director and attended the Mamut Art Project. Her large-scale pencil drawings were then featured in several group exhibitions, and she also held her first solo exhibition "Flowers of the Night" in 2019.

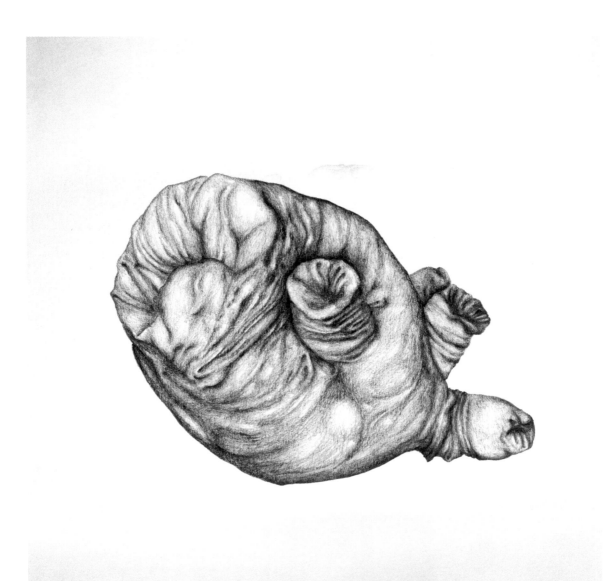

Candan İşcan

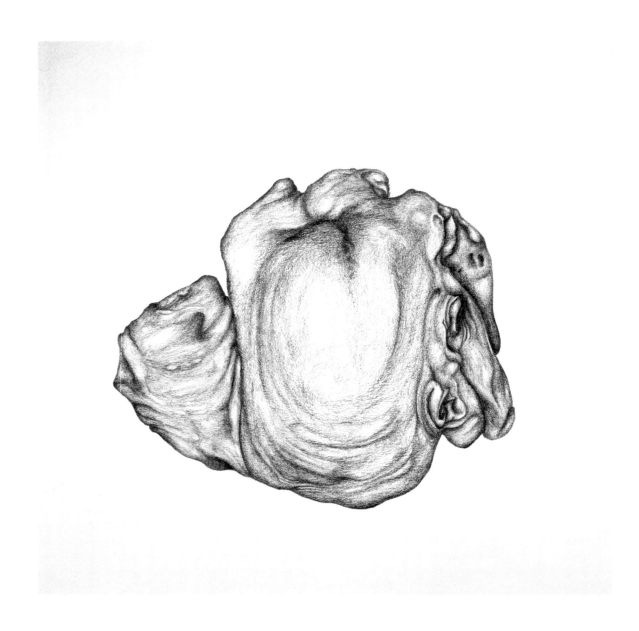

GRAPHITE

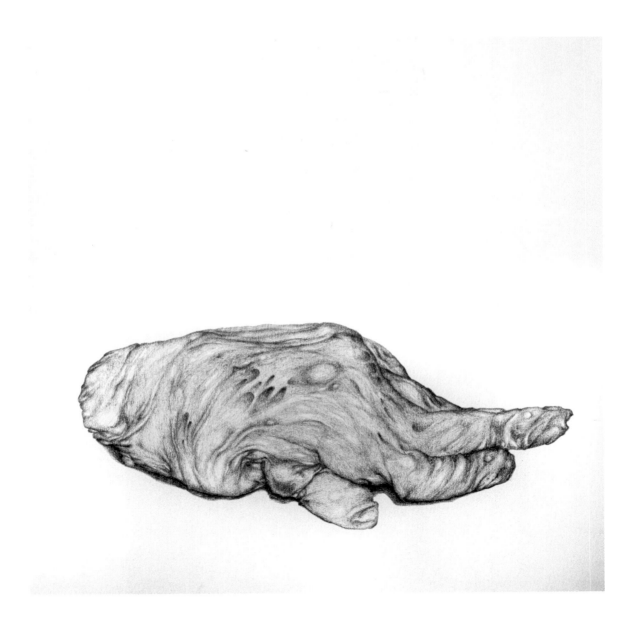

Candan İşcan

GRAPHITE

Memento Vivere I
700 mm x 1000 mm

054

Candan İşcan

Candan İşcan

JUDY CHEN

Judy Chen is a designer and illustrator working in branding and scientific illustration. She was born in Hong Kong and now lives in the Netherlands. She is passionate about translating scientific data into poetic visuals and she sees imagery as a powerful and effective medium for conveying complex stories.

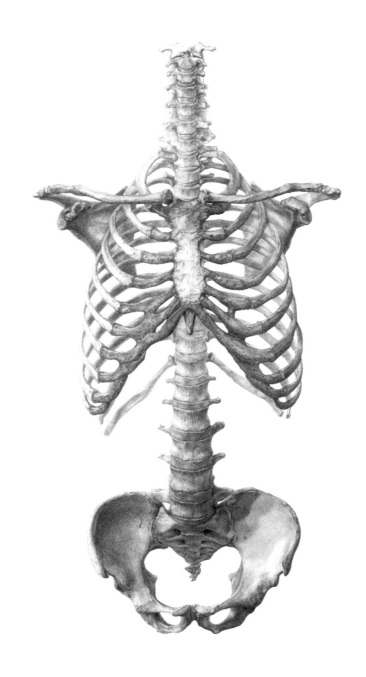

Judy Chen

The Human Skeleton
594 mm x 841 mm

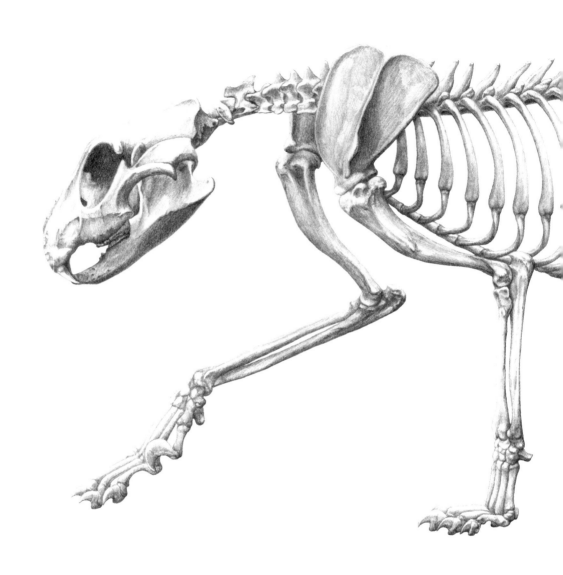

GRAPHITE

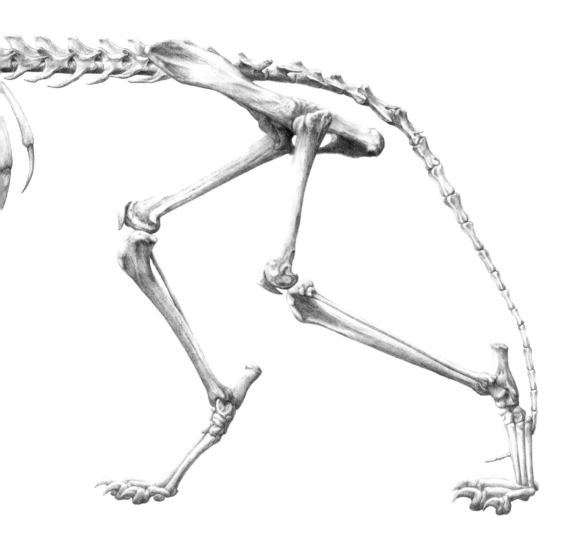

Judy Chen

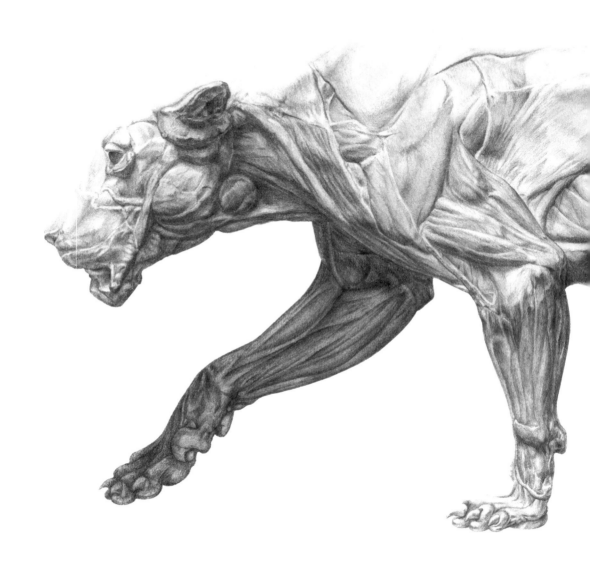

Judy Chen

Muscular Systems of Panthera Leo
594 mm x 841 mm

063

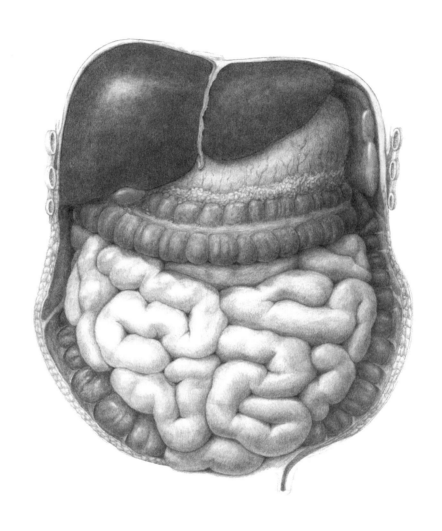

The Human Abdomen I
420 mm x 594 mm

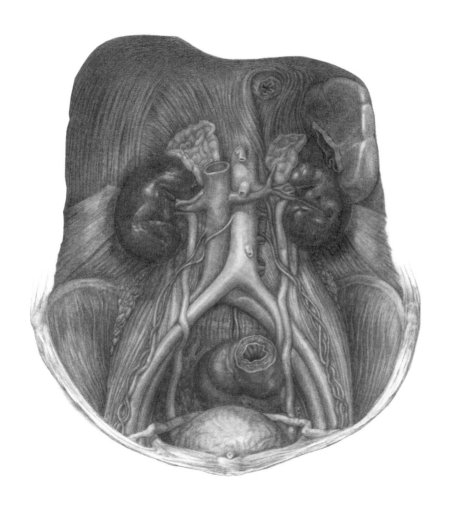

Judy Chen

The Human Abdomen II
420 mm x 594 mm

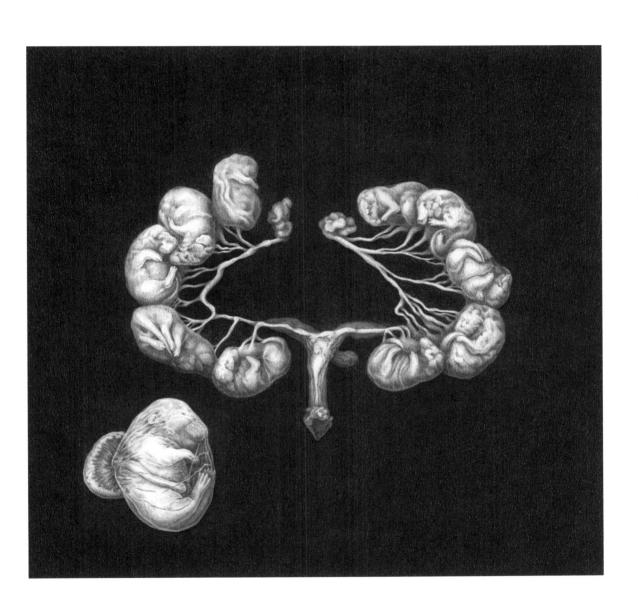

Judy Chen

DELPHINE MONIEZ

Delphine Moniez graduated from The Beaux-Arts de Paris in 2011 with a focus on drawing. She has taken part in several group shows at "Le 6B dessine son salon" and the Biennale d'Issy "Paysages, pas si sages." Her work was exhibited at the Biennale du Dessin Actuel Grafia in Saint-Affrique, and at Anne+ Art Contemporain in Paris.

Delphine Moniez

Untitled (2 February 2019)
148 mm x 210 mm

069

GRAPHITE

Untitled (2016)
1000 mm x 700 mm

070

Delphine Moniez

Untitled (March 2018)
500 mm x 640 mm

Delphine Moniez

Untitled (31 March 2021)
550 mm x 750 mm

Delphine Moniez

Untitled (April 2020)
750 mm x 540 mm

075

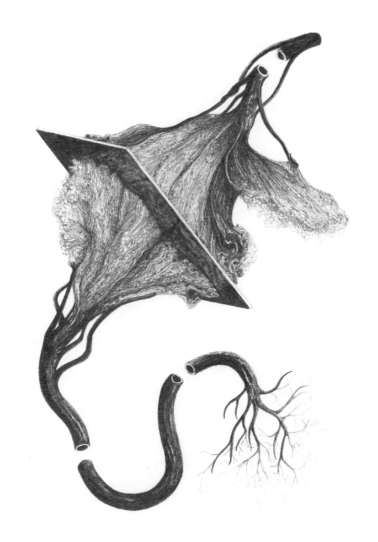

Untitled (11 january 2022)
297 mm x 210 mm

Delphine Moniez

Untitled (15 january 2022)
297 mm x 210 mm

CHIEN-FAN LIU

Chien-Fan Liu is an illustrator and comic artist based in Taiwan. Her works include posters, animations for musicians, and editorial illustrations. Aside from commissioned works, she creates personal comic art and has been selected for the Jeune Talent contest in 2020. She also won second prize in the Digital Challenge of Angoulême International Comic Festival in 2018.

Chien-Fan Liu

Excerpt from "That Night"
219 mm x 297 mm

Untitled
219 mm x 297 mm

Chien-Fan Liu

In the Mountains
297 mm x 421 mm

GRAPHITE

Ritual
219 mm x 297 mm

082

Chien-Fan Liu

Witches
297 mm x 421 mm

083

Chien-Fan Liu

Hibernate in Summer
219 mm x 297 mm

DIMITRIS ANASTASIOU

Dimitris Anastasiou studied painting at the Athens School of Fine Arts, and has presented his paintings in three solo shows, as well as over 50 group exhibitions and international art fairs in Greece and various countries across Europe in collaboration with Kaplanon Galleries. He also published the graphic novel "A=-A' in both English and Greek.

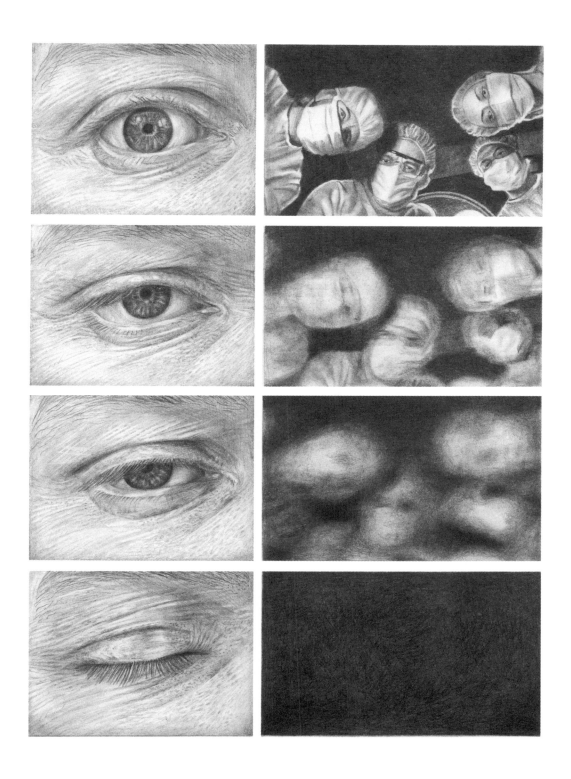

Dimitris Anastasiou

Surgery I (A Page From "A=-A')
350 mm x 260 mm

087

Dimitris Anastasiou

My Dream to Fly Has Become a Dream
(A Page From "A=-A'), 350 mm x 700 mm

En anarchie nv o Argos

GRAPHITE

Dimitris Anastasiou

In the Beginning was the World
500 mm x 700 mm

Dimitris Anastasiou

Wandering (A Page From "A=-A')
260 mm x 360 mm

MISAO IWAMOTO

After obtaining a BA in Literature in Japan, Misao Iwamoto moved to Belgium to study visual arts and graphic design. She is a graphic designer, drawing tutor, and illustrator. Iwamoto mainly uses graphite pencils for her extremely delicate visual storytelling. The inspiration for her work often lies in books, movies, photography, philosophy, and true stories.

Misao Iwamoto

Those Left Behind #2
140 mm x 110 mm

GRAPHITE

Fall Landscape
135 mm x 115 mm

098

Misao Iwamoto

Missing Pieces
210 mm x 165 mm

099

GRAPHITE

Those Left Behind
160 mm x 150 mm

100

Misao Iwamoto

Narcissus
170 mm x 130 mm

Missing Pieces #2
155 mm x 105 mm

Misao Iwamoto

Hiding from the World
180 mm x 135 mm

NATALIA KULKA

Natalia Kulka is a Warsaw-based illustrator who graduated from the Academy of Fine Arts in Kraków. She co-created "Zeszyt", a series of publications about drawing, and the artbook "Jobs and Works" as part of the Dream Team art group. She also illustrates for net journal "Studia Litteraria et Historica". In 2019, she held her solo show in the House of Culture in Warsaw.

Natalia Kulka

The Glow
117 mm x 131 mm

GRAPHITE

The Saint
137 mm x 140 mm

106

Natalia Kulka

The Boy
207 mm x 185 mm

Begonia
80 mm x 110 mm

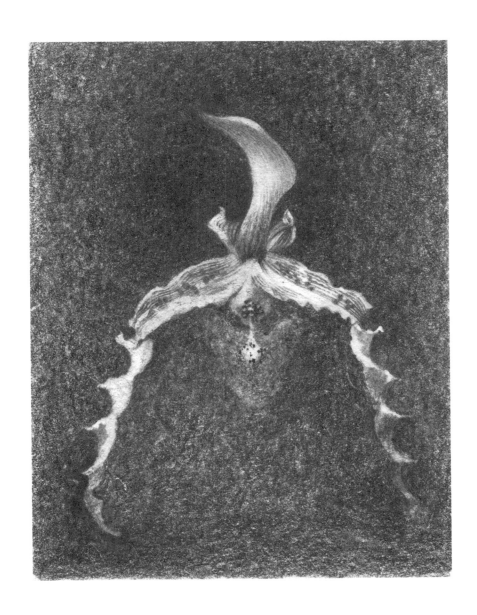

Natalia Kulka

Orchid
85 mm x 112 mm

GRAPHITE

The Varnish
173 mm x 213 mm

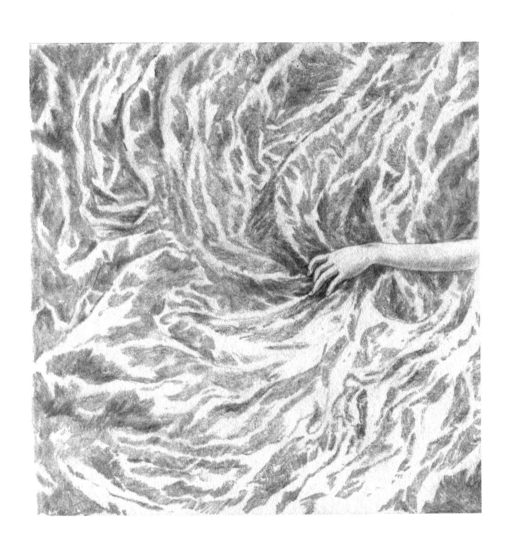

Natalia Kulka

The Hand and/or the Landcape
138 mm x 148 mm

HALO

halo is a Fukushima-based artist who draws mainly with pencils. Ghosts, smoke, and tiny flowers are common themes in halo's work.

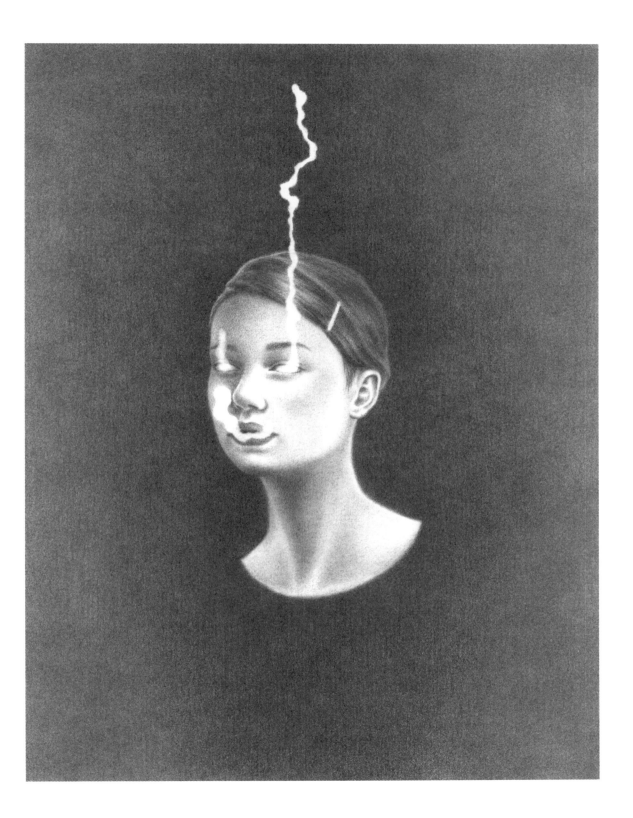

halo

Untitled
302 mm x 241 mm

Funeral for a Friend
302 mm x 247 mm

halo

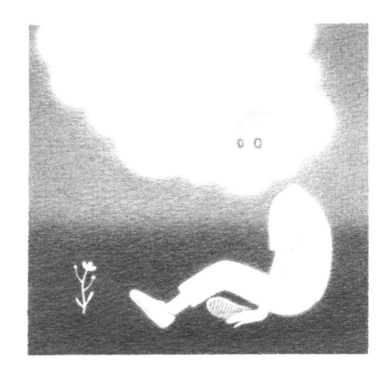

Windless Day
200 mm x 200 mm

Windless Day
200 mm x 200 mm

Whereabouts of Smoke
199 mm x 199 mm

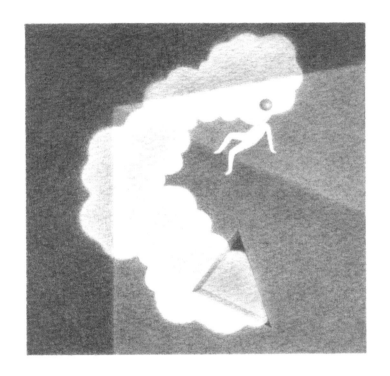

Whereabouts of Smoke
199 mm x 199 mm

ADAM LIAM ROSE

Adam Liam Rose is an interdisciplinary artist working across sculpture, installation, video and drawing. Born in Jerusalem and raised mostly in the United States, his works investigate the aesthetic systems of power embedded within architecture. Exploring the politics of "safety" in Israel / Palestine and the United States, Rose's practice looks to structures of separation and control.

Adam Liam Rose

Stages of Fallout (scrim)
190.5 mm x 279.4 mm

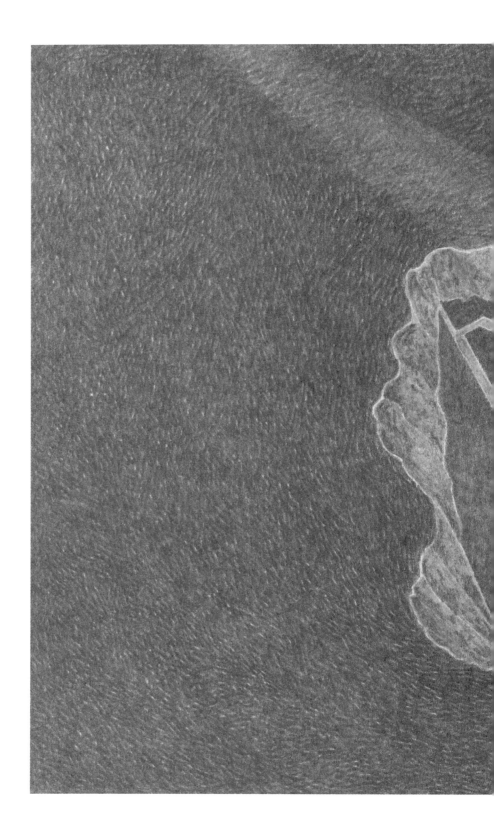

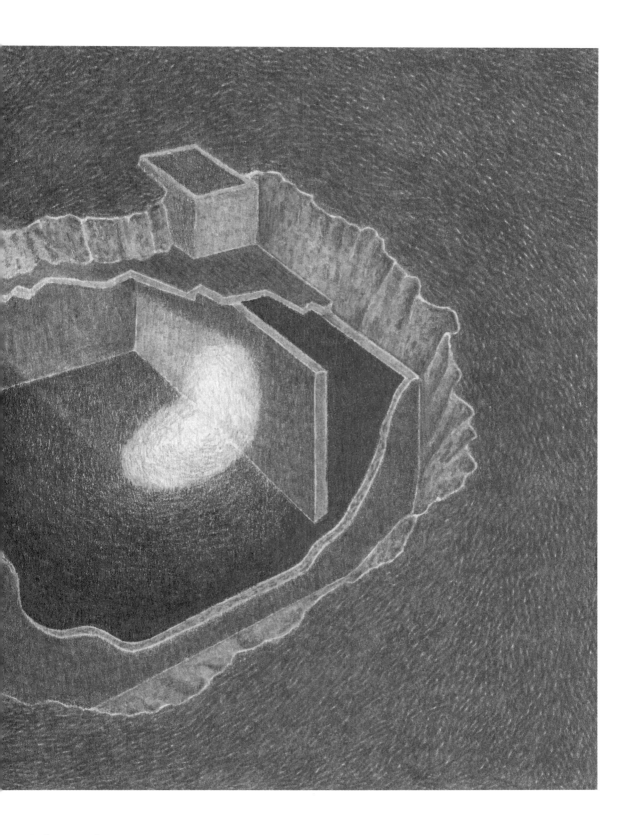

Adam Liam Rose

Stages of Fallout (see the light)
190.5 mm x 279.4 mm

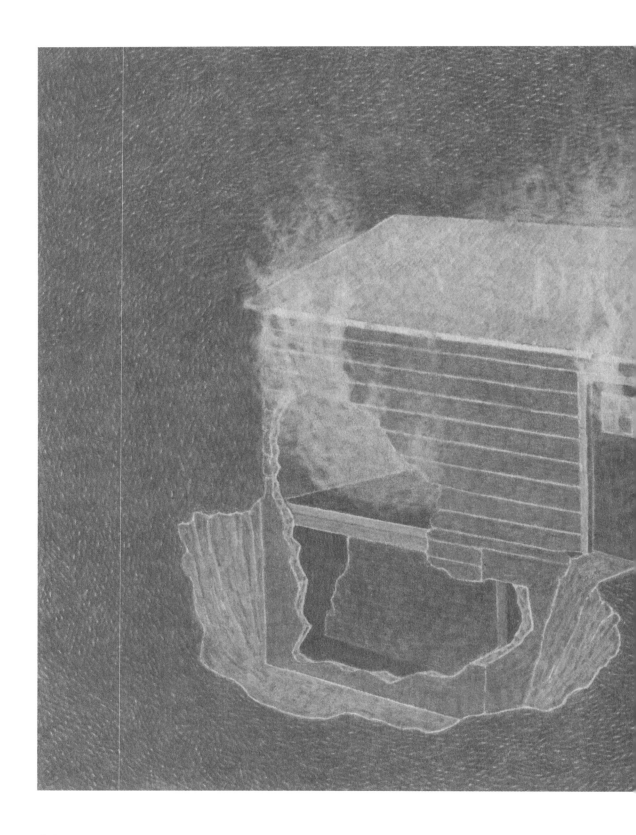

GRAPHITE

Stages of Fallout (burning house)
190.5 mm x 279.4 mm

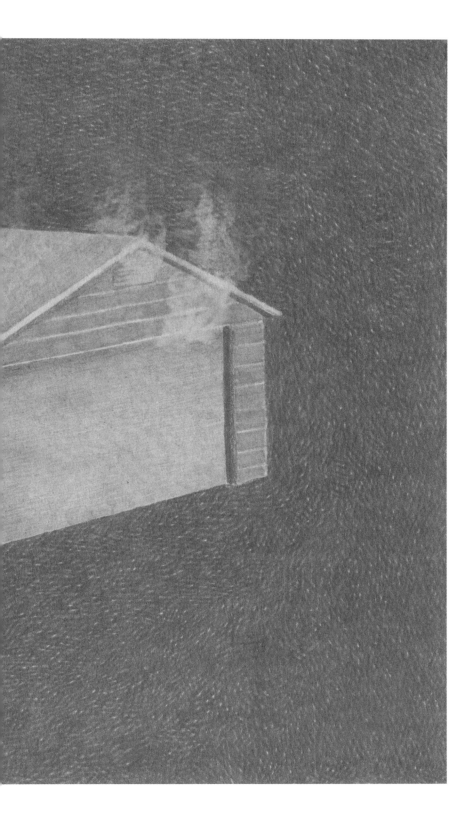

Adam Liam Rose

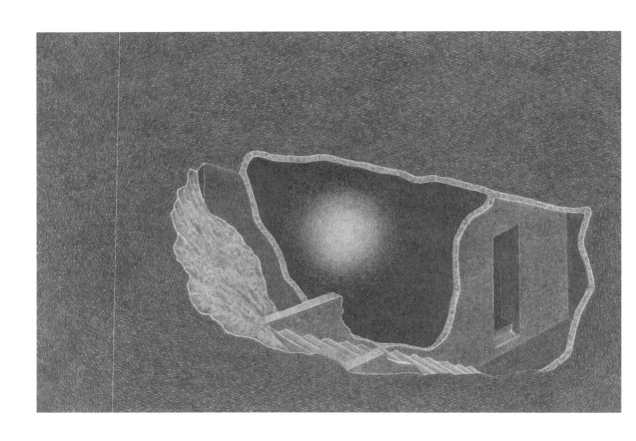

GRAPHITE

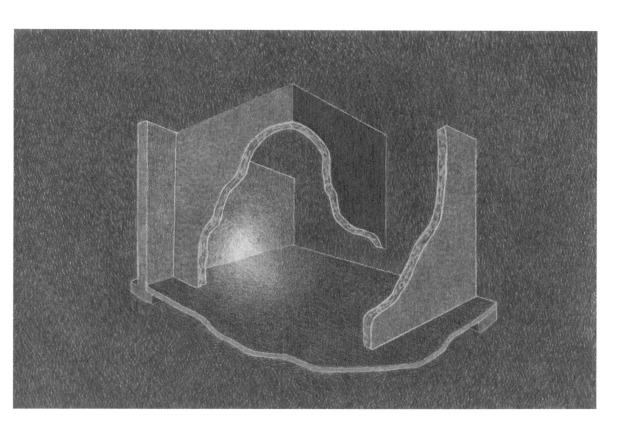

Adam Liam Rose

GRAPHITE

Stages of Fallout (never lonely)
279.4 mm x 355.6 mm

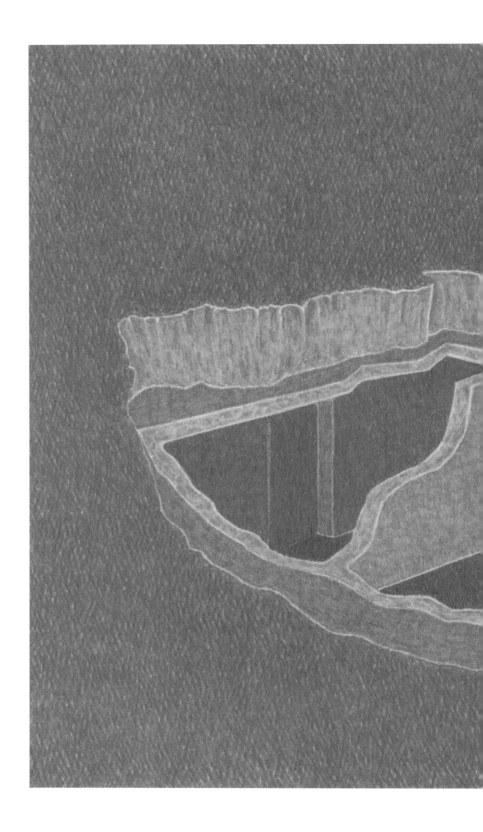

Adam Liam Rose

Stages of Fallout (labyrinth)
190.5 mm x 279.4 mm

JON BOBBY BENJAMIN

Jon Bobby studied art at Brandeis and VCU. He lives and works in Philadelphia. His recent work have primarily been in graphite and mixed media on paper.

Jon Bobby Benjamin

Dying Gaul
250 mm x 200 mm

135

Jon Bobby Benjamin

Dog Bite
250 mm x 200 mm

GRAPHITE

Hammer Lost in Weeds Gone to
Hammer Heaven, 250 mm x 200 mm

Jon Bobby Benjamin

Nailed Flower
250 mm x 200 mm

JULIA PŁOCH

Julia Płoch is an animator and illustrator who graduated from the Academy Of Fine Arts in Kraków. She is always interested in showing stories in a visual way, and creates comics, illustrations, backgrounds for games, and short animations. Her works are often dark, but with a touch of grotesque humour.

Julia Płoch

Egg
210 mm x 297 mm

Julia Płoch

He Pees in Her Eye
210 mm x 297 mm

143

GRAPHITE

Somebody Help!
210 mm x 297 mm

Julia Płoch

GRAPHITE

Cocoon
210 mm x 297 mm

146

Julia Płoch

No Title
210 mm x 297 mm

PAULINE RIVEAUX GOLOUBINOW

Pauline Riveaux Goloubinow is a painter and engraver. She had her first solo show in the Gallery Von Kraft in 2009 after being discovered as an exchange student in Berlin. She has won several awards for her drawing and printmaking work. Pauline's work explores the theme of tension through the choices of lighting applied to subjects in a poetic way.

Pauline Riveaux Goloubinow   La Règle du Je
120 mm x 105 mm

Pauline Riveaux Goloubinow

Daddy Found a Place
120 mm x 165 mm

Le Jeu du Précipice
200 mm x 300 mm

Pauline Riveaux Goloubinow

Baba Yaga
120 mm x 160 mm

GRAPHITE

Pauline Riveaux Goloubinow

Ado les sens
120 mm x 160 mm

WENYI GENG

Wenyi is a Chinese illustrator and storyteller. Born in Japan, Wenyi studied illustration in New York and can speak Chinese, Japanese and English. However, she still thinks that art is the best language to express and communicate one's feelings with. She currently lives in Tokyo and spends time in her riverside studio drawing things and telling stories.

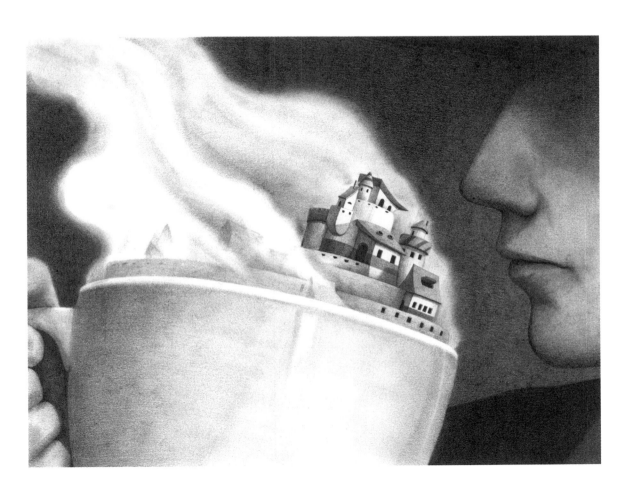

Wenyi Geng

Afternoon Tea
279.4 mm x 355.6 mm

Wenyi Geng

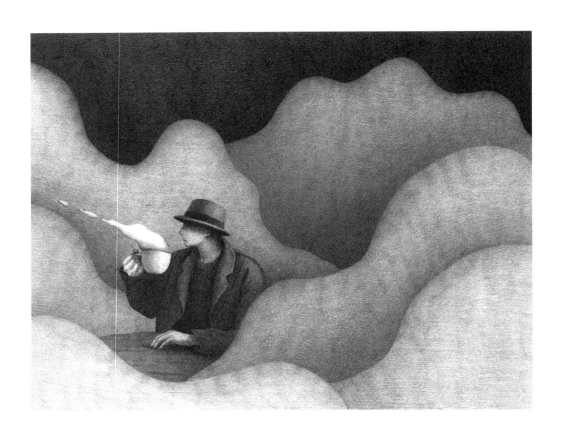

GRAPHITE

Afternoon Tea
279.4 mm x 355.6 mm

160

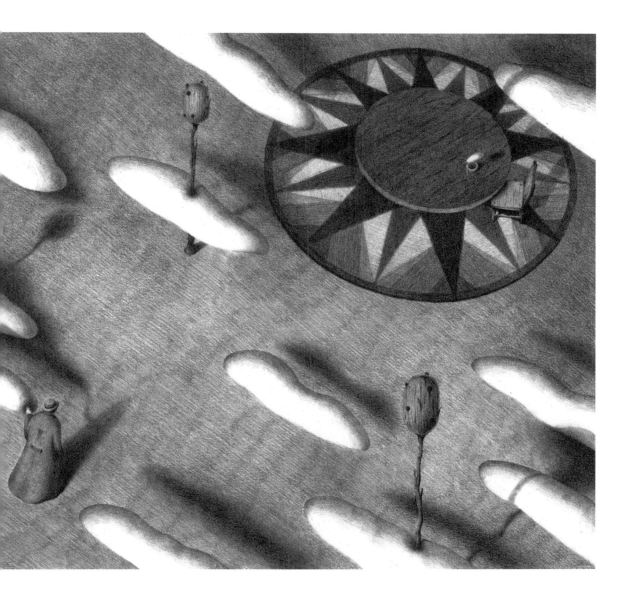

Wenyi Geng

Afternoon Tea
279.4 mm x 355.6 mm

Afternoon Tea
279.4 mm x 355.6 mm

Wenyi Geng

KAI GIETZEN

Kai Gietzen is an artist and illustrator in his senior year at the Rhode Island School of Design. He grew up in Milwaukee, Wisconsin and often draws from memory and imagination to create works in digital and traditional media. In addition, he loves learning about science, natural history, and various folklore traditions.

Kai Gietzen

Adaptation III
177.33 mm x 200.53 mm

GRAPHITE

The Peppered Moth
133 mm x 190 mm

Kai Gietzen

Adaptation I
160.74 mm x 157.1 mm

Kai Gietzen

Adaptation II
159.22 mm x 127.25 mm

ISABEL CAVENECIA

Isabel Cavenecia is a Peruvian/Dutch artist. She completed her Bachelor of Fine Arts at the Royal Academy of Fine Arts, The Hague in 2014. Known for her sensitive graphite and pastel drawings, Isabel has exhibited her works at several galleries and museums such as FOAM, Kunstenhuis, TAC, and 8 Salon.

Isabel Cavenecia

My Ancestors in a Square Box
420 mm x 260 mm

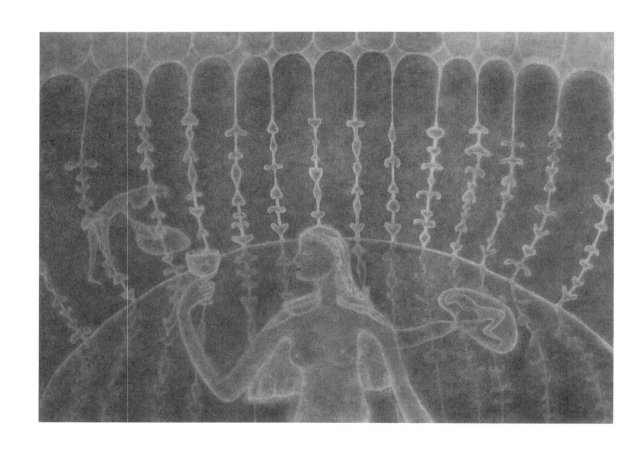

A Cup of Fresh Water
590 mm x 840 mm

Isabel Cavenecia

173

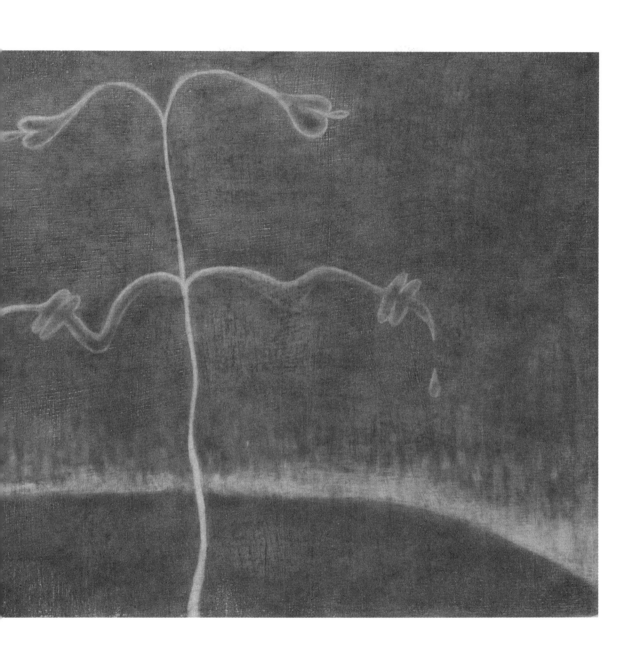

Isabel Cavenecia

Burning Ring of Fire
220 mm x 490 mm

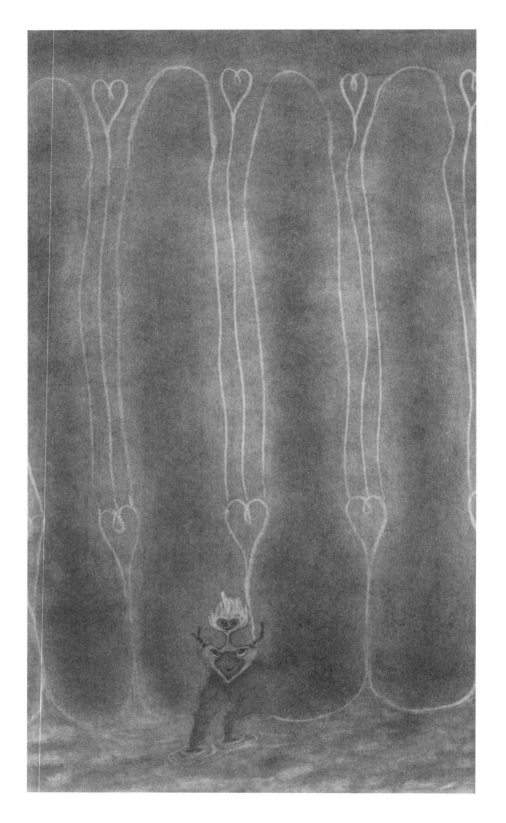

GRAPHITE

Hello
240 mm x 440 mm

Isabel Cavenecia

Two Ladies Traveling at Night
420 mm x 360 mm

177

KYOUNG-MI AHN

Seoul-based illustrator Kyoung-Mi Ahn explores the possibilities in the materiality of reading and book structures. After receiving an MA from Kingston University in illustration, she published two picture books and illustrated 15 books. Kyoung-Mi has won illustration awards at the Bologna Bookfair, the Incentive Award at the Sharjah Reading Festival, the second prize at the CICLA exhibition, and the Merit Award at the 3x3 Show.

Kyoung-Mi Ahn

Blackbird
297 mm x 420 mm

179

Blackbird
297 mm x 420 mm

Kyoung-Mi Ahn

Blackbird
297 mm x 420 mm

GRAPHITE

Moongazing Journey
420 mm x 297 mm

182

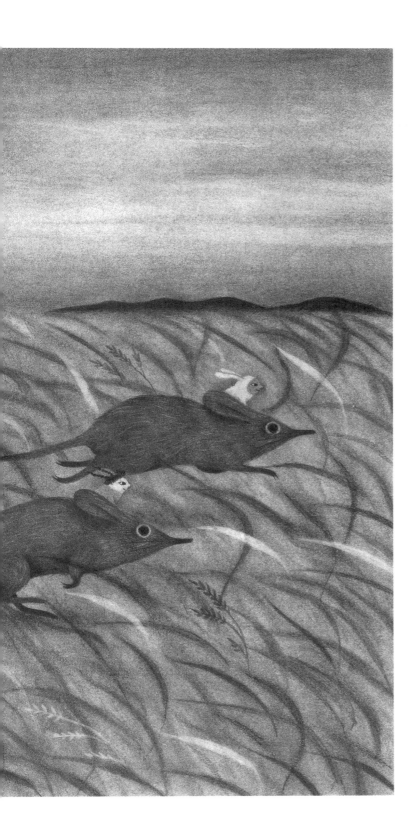

Kyoung-Mi Ahn

GRAPHITE

Blackbird
297 mm x 420 mm

Kyoung-Mi Ahn

Blackbird
297 mm x 420 mm

CARLOS FERNANDEZ

Born in Madrid in 1980, it wasn't until 30 years later that Carlos Fernandez started drawing. Specialising in pencil drawing, his art describes mysterious atmospheres with a surreal and dark theme through which Carlos represents dreams and feelings. He always tries to tell a story with an open end for different interpretations to involve the viewer.

Carlos Fernandez

Home
193 mm x 245 mm

187

GRAPHITE

Plague
170 mm x 220 mm

Carlos Fernandez

Fossilized
209 mm x 209 mm

The Loop Man
208 mm x 215 mm

Carlos Fernandez

The Empty Man
210 mm x 279 mm

GRAPHITE

The Exchanger
209 mm x 243 mm

Carlos Fernandez

Under Construction
190 mm x 228 mm

193

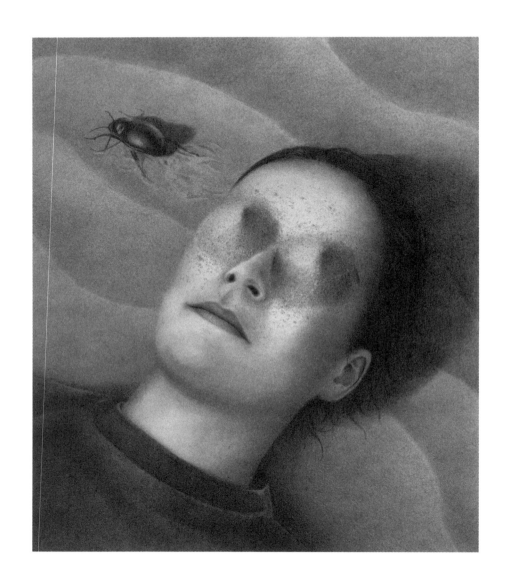

Enigma
170 mm x 203 mm

Carlos Fernandez

Desolation
187 mm x 233 mm

OIMIZI

In 2019, oimizi graduated from SI Picture Book School in Seoul and mainly focuses on creating images with the pencil. In 2020, the artist published "Monstruosaedition group dessin" in France, and is currently working on a picture book project at Some Books.

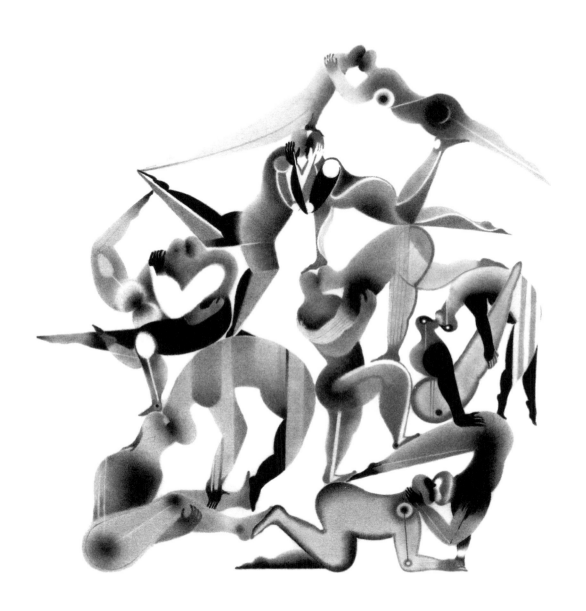

oimizi

Warm Composition
280 x 310 mm

oimizi

Graceful Ghost
297 mm x 210 mm

Island (Book Project) /06
280 mm x 310 mm

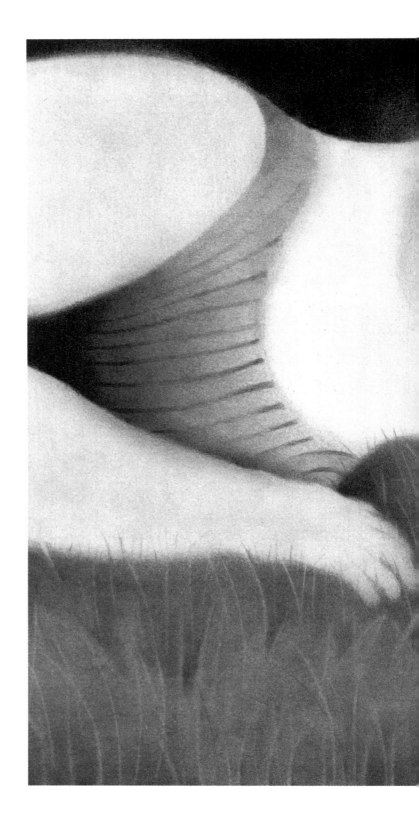

oimizi

Graceful Ghost
297 mm x 210 mm

MARIBEL FLÓREZ

Born in 1988, Maribel Flórez studied art at the Universidad de Nacional de Colombia with a focus on graphite. Maribel's works go beyond the hyper-reality and transform the simple places of everyday life into a space inhabited in bidimensionality, permeated by the emotional charge of her universe.

Maribel Flórez

11:00 p.m.
260 mm x 210 mm

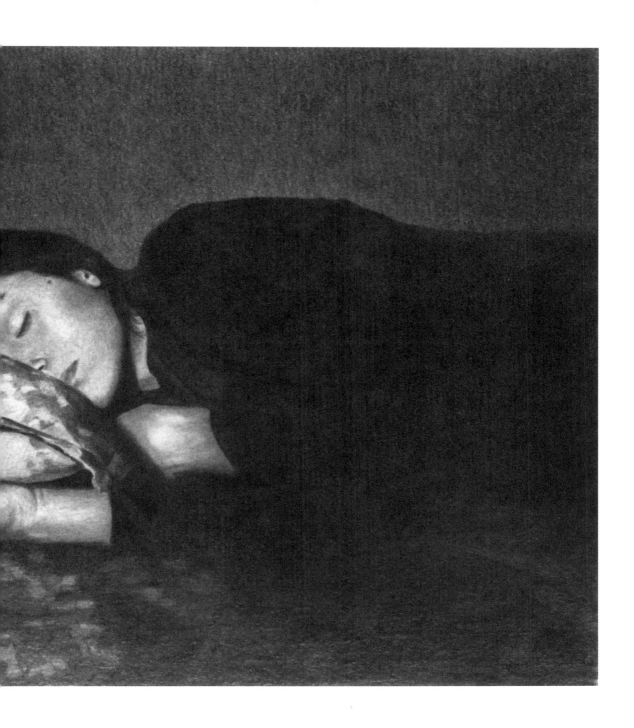

Maribel Flórez

Noche
130 mm x 220 mm

Baño
210 mm x 130 mm

Maribel Flórez

Barbie
280 mm x 210 mm

Maribel Flórez

Cuarto de Julieta
130 mm x 210 mm

En Agua
260 mm x 210 mm

Maribel Flórez

Sombra
130 mm x 210 mm

JONO DRY

Based in Cape Town and entirely self taught, South African artist Jono Dry has worked for the last thirteen years on creating a practice centred around his large-scale hyperrealist graphite works that take over 2 months to complete. Exhibiting both locally and internationally, Dry has devoted his practice to pushing the medium of graphite.

Jono Dry

Nurtured Nature (Male)
1640 mm x 1140 mm

215

GRAPHITE

Figure in Frame
1640 mm x 1140 mm

Jono Dry

Berkana
800 mm x 1140 mm

Sanctuary
800 mm x 1140 mm

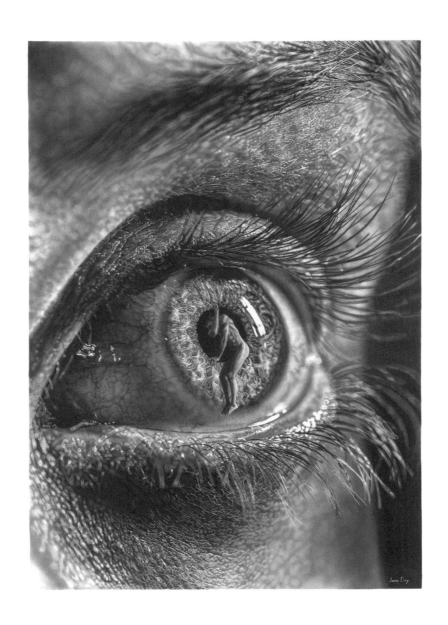

Jono Dry

Pupil
1640 mm x 1140 mm

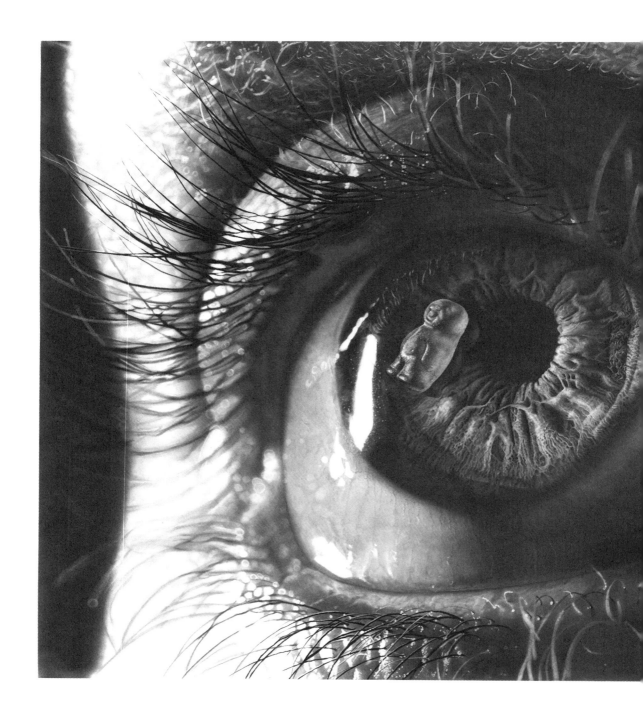

GRAPHITE

Gummy Bear and Eye
1140 mm x 1640 mm

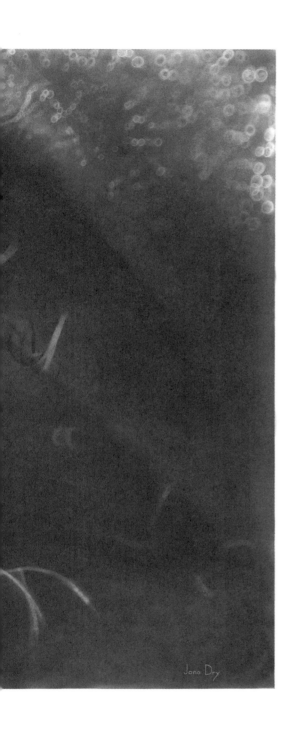

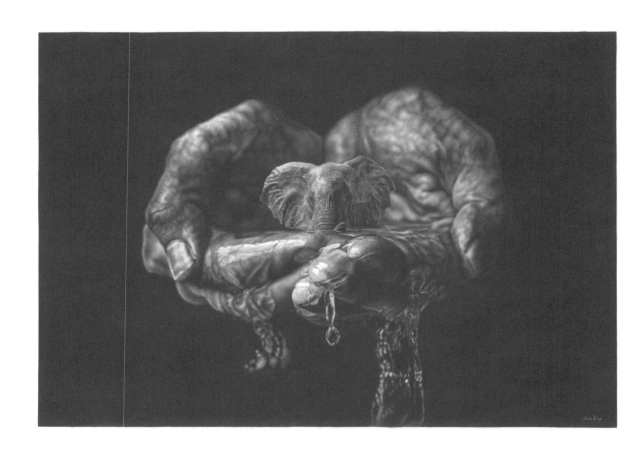

GRAPHITE

Handle
1140 mm x 1640 mm

222

Jono Dry

Ruin
800 mm x 1140 mm

223

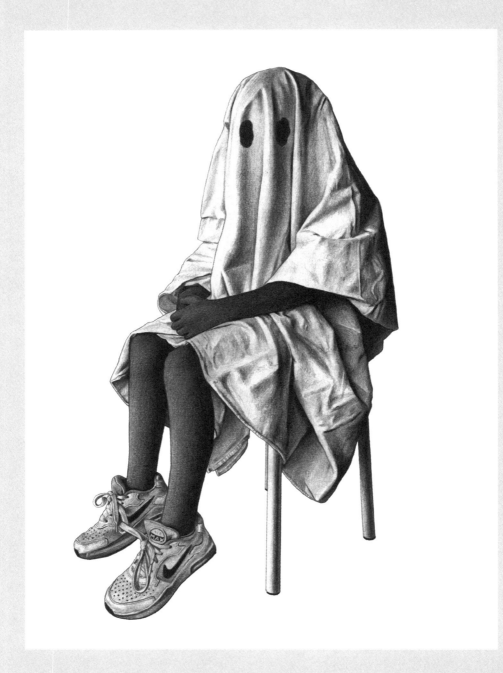

ARTIST TALK

Air Max
300 mm x 400 mm

AMANDINE URRUTY

———

WHY A COLOURLESS WORLD CAN STILL BE A COMPELLING ONE

Amandine Urruty

Never Again
1500 mm x 1000 mm

Although she professes to work from the comfort of her bed, Amandine Urruty's imagination is never at rest. Armed with a suitcase full of pen(cil)s by her side, the French artist likens the curious characters she conceives to ones you too could create while wandering through the local flea market — a unique mishmash of human characteristics and objects that make for delightfully deviant portraits. Growing up in a small rural town, Urruty's creative journey was a colourful one driven by her love of art and learning, coming into her own through a variety of influences over the years.

"My parents were not interested in painting(s) at all — in fact, the only artwork we had at home was a Salvador Dali poster in our toilet! — but my passion for art was always evident. In finding a way to learn more on the subject, the tiny library in my hometown became my go-to resource. There, I discovered Magritte, Bosch, and a French comic artist called Edika, who became my very first 'master' at the age of 12. Drawn to the grotesque characters and over-the-top characteristics he is known for, I unscrupulously copied his style for a while until I became 16 and my dream came true at last: when I got the chance to move to a bigger city and study art in university."

"I felt like a backpacker in a brand new world there and fell in love with so many artists — David, Ingres, Francis Bacon, Pierre & Gilles, Joel-Peter Witkin, Cindy Sherman... Those were some thrilling times! I loved absolutely everything that was labelled 'art' and gorged on it all. After dabbling in photography, I came back to Flemish painting — with Bruegel, Patinir, Memling. I love Renaissance art as much as contemporary art and continue to have a voracious appetite for it. Today, I try to go to shows as often as I can, where my favourite art pieces are often bizarre and big works of graphite."

Like many artists, Urruty explored several techniques and mediums of expression over time to arrive at her distinct style. During a difficult stretch in her life,

Amandine Urruty was born in 1982 and is currently based in Paris and Toulous. After receiving her Master of Philosophy in Art in 2005, Urruty began exhibiting her work and working as an illustrator. Her illustrations have been exhibited in galleries throughout Europe, North America, and Asia. She has published two books, Robinet d'Amour (2011) and Dommage Fromage (2014).

Amandine Urruty

From the Cave
300 mm x 400 mm

she even experimented with bright colours, in part upon the suggestion of others around her, but ended up going back to graphite — something she has always loved for the way it reminds her of drawing classes back in university, as well as the endless possibilities it presents due to the material's radical but fundamental qualities. She is also fascinated by black and grey, in particular, the colours' rich history, the sense of depth they can be utilised to form, and the sobriety they evoke. She cites the chiaroscuro process as one of the most magical things she knows, finding excitement in both creating and seeing an illusion.

"I used to love copying David, Ingres, and Michel-Ange with my pencils — there was such an oldfashioned charm to doing so. Although my first artworks were also in black and white, they are slightly different from my recent ones. Drawn in pen, they were more rough and less precise, with less lines and gradations. At the time, I swore I would never, ever use colour, but changed my mind a year later in 2009, partly because people kept asking: 'what about colour?'. That's how I entered my 'magical thinking' phase of producing very colourful pictures with fluorescent pencils."

"Looking back now, it was my child-like way of coping with a sad chapter in my life. I fully immersed myself in candy pink and neon blue for two years, producing enough drawings to publish a 128-page book. After my dad's death, I needed to find new energy, which is how I went back to black and white once and for all, as a statement of sorts. I had to cling onto something essential and leave the frivolous behind me. Most and foremost, I wanted to learn how to draw again. Unlike some artists who needed to 'unlearn' to reach a type of essentialist simplicity, I wanted to work on mastering my tool, like a craftswoman. It was a challenging period, so I had to choose a challenging medium. Back then, I thought I would never be able to handle graphite correctly — it was too dirty, too demanding, and too intimidating, having seen the works of the super-talented artists before me; but I had to try."

When it comes to her creative process, Urruty thinks she subconsciously puts her dreams to paper sometimes, even though she never remembers them. After filling her notebook with bits and pieces of ideas, she tries out different compositions through rough sketches before connecting the dots to develop the theme underlining her work. She finds this to be a freeing way to combine characteristics and objects towards the building of the whole picture step by step — from the first big blocks in the initial sketches to the little details at the end on the final canvas.

"In terms of inspiration, most of my work is connected to my emotions and sentiments, be they the disappointments and

Amandine Urruty

Floral Ghost
800 mm x 800 mm

day-to-day nonsense I had to deal with in my childhood or my memories, fears, regrets, and joy today. I liken my work to the construction of exquisite cadavers guided by a theme. Just as one would expect in a surrealistic mental labyrinth, it features odd meetings and mixtures of genres and references, as I love experimenting with random combinations. To quote Lautréamont, my work is 'the chance encounter of a sewing machine and an umbrella on an operating table'. In making the bizarre bloom, I use masks and costumes as tools to create uncanny feelings. Although I resonate with each of my art pieces for this reason, my favourite ones are often the 'bigger' ones in terms of size or technical ambition. Then again, as I seem to suffer from some sort of 'chronic dissatisfaction', I also often defer to the last drawing I made, until the next one takes its place."

As she looks ahead to an exciting future, Urruty reminisces about a time in her past when she never thought she would become an artist due to perceptions that it would be hard to make a living. However, having built her career through illustrations and murals, as well as over 70 exhibitions around the world and four monographic books in her name to date, she no longer feels this way — but understands how it can be hard for aspiring creatives to take the leap. Ultimately, while everybody's journey is different, she believes that hard work is key while staying true to oneself.

"Although I had no idea of what an artist's life would be like, it was simply a big 'no-no' at the time, which is why I stayed at my university for eight years in an attempt to become an art teacher. However, as work became more theoretical and boring, I felt like I had to take a risk. This is where chance entered the picture. I began singing in a band with friends and, even though I was an awful vocalist, it inspired me to create my first posters, record covers, t-shirts, etc. I then began to receive positive feedback about my drawings until a gallery eventually offered to host my first show, setting me on my new path as an illustrator. Although this happened years ago, I do not regret any of it."

"At the end of the day, I believe that anything is possible and, even though this sounds like a cliché, I would advise up-and-coming artists to work. A lot. Do not spare any effort or think you have 'made it'. The road ahead is long, perilous, and full of surprises, but it is important to be lucid and rigorous. Keep on working and progressing! Drawing is such a time-consuming activity and while I personally

prefer to focus on the production of original pieces, I recently began to experiment with ceramics and it has been pretty exciting! There may be something there in the future, but most importantly, when people ask me 'what about colour?' today, I can sincerely answer – 'never again'."

Amandine Urruty

Self Portrait as a Clown
300 mm x 400 mm

Amandine Urruty

Landscapes
700 mm x 1000 mm

The Woods
700 mm x 1000 mm

Amandine Urruty

Glitters
700 mm x 1000 mm

DUKHOON GIM

DRAWING DREAMLIKE TAKES ON FILMS AND THE FAMILIAR

Dukhoon Gim

Willow
1050 mm x 748 mm

Dukhoon Gim

Indifferentiable Point
748 mm x 1051 mm

Inspiration comes in many forms and can be found in the most unlikely of places, whether it is deliberately sought or not. One might stumble upon it during a quiet evening walk in the woods, where all is still except for the crunching of footsteps on fallen leaves and the occasional birdsong

piercing the air. For some, it jolts them awake in the middle of a cold shower or between the first sips of coffee in the morning. Many have gleaned it from the melody of a favourite song, works of art from a different time, or the words of authors who likely went through similar processes of exploration for ideas and meaning. Be it from a familiar or unfamiliar source, inspiration is personal — as are the distinct creative outcomes borne out of it.

Today, the proliferation of digital content and social media means inspiration is only a few clicks away. Coupled with the more advanced tools available for artists and designers to express themselves, the world is currently teeming with projects that showcase a variety of techniques, influences, and subjects that tickle the imagination. Amid this confluence of creativity,

Dukhoon Gim's graphite work is a breath of fresh air with its delightful juxtaposition of classic medium and contemporary inspiration, as he skilfully brings together elements from the East and the West.

Hailing from South Korea, Gim is among the many creatives breathing life and diversity into Seoul's thriving art scene, which was propelled by the great post-Olympics boom in the 2000s. Buoyed by the Korean wave or 'hallyu' brought about by Korean dramas and movies such as Train to Busan and Parasite, the city is now home to many galleries and venues that attract a variety of international exhibitors, collectors, and enthusiasts, bringing together talent from all over the globe. It is an exciting time for local artists, emerging or otherwise, as they draw inspiration from new energy and exposure while carving out their own spaces through passion, dedication, and resourcefulness.

Amid this buzz, Gim has been quietly making waves with his unique art. After building a career as a graphic designer for 9 years, he switched to a slightly different path — participating in his first group show in 2014. According to Mimi Park of Thomas Park Gallery, Gim "captures a dreamlike world of extraordinary sensitivity with a subtle, humorous touch" — and it shows through the masterful way with which he wields his pencils. From natural settings with a fantastical touch to snapshots from one's daily routine like having breakfast and waiting for the lift, each piece invites the viewer in for a closer inspection, often rewarding them with a little surprise.

His Weeping Willow series, for example, features the elegant trees in a textural wonderland on canvas — at once beautiful and ominous, punctuated by quirky or blink-and-you-miss-it details like a woman on a blow-up dolphin, a sinking car, or a tiny homage to Pink Floyd's 'Wish You Were Here'. Interestingly, there are men in suits in several of his other artworks, such as Agents, Isn't It Real, and Indifferentiable Point, who do not look particularly out of place, given their surroundings. Every bold and delicate stroke is thoughtfully marked, culminating in monochromatic gems.

Gim's journey with graphite began with a simple goal: to work with the most basic materials he could use. When asked about his reason for using the medium and what makes it the best in his eyes, he says, "Graphite has the aura of being a pure substance as well as a medium for drawing." It is a duality he is fascinated by and an idea he is trying to get across more effectively with every new piece he works on, as he endeavours to "create objects made out of a single material by omitting differences in colour". His numeral series ('40…73…') is a testament to this, showcasing organic 3D-like blocks along grids that resemble city maps from a distant planet.

When it comes to his creative process, Gim takes about a month to complete a 1052 mm x 750 mm-sized canvas. Although he admits to rarely listening to music these days and surfs the Internet for inspiration, he is particularly drawn to movies. Whether you are a film buff or not, there are many ways with which a movie can inspire, regardless of genre. From cult flicks with compelling stories that make us

Dukhoon Gim worked as a graphic designer for nine years, and participated in a group exhibition as an artist for the first time in 2014. Up until now, he has held a total of six individual exhibitions.

think and feel-good movies that remind us to be more compassionate to the latest blockbusters which feature cutting-edge technology, one can almost-always find something deeper to resonate with on top of immersing in the visual spectacle unfolding on screen.

Gim is no stranger to these qualities: "I watch one or two movies every day. Movies are life to me — and are other worlds in themselves. It is not easy to pick a favourite because I enjoy so many, but I do like 'Blade Runner', 'Ferris Bueller's Day Off' and Wong Kar-Wai's films from the 1990s very much." In fact, he sees pieces from the afore-mentioned Weeping Willow series as movie stills that symbolise "seeds of undefined meaning", while his portraits are also inspired by scenes from old Hollywood classics, in which he depicts the subjects as stone statues to reflect the fact that "past moments may be forgotten but still exist as part of time".

While the beauty of nature has been a big source of inspiration in Korean art and literature for many years, the way with which Gim merges landscapes with modern elements makes his hyper-realistic scenarios all his own. Although he cites David Shrigley and Raymond Pettibone as artists he admires, Gim looks to the books he is reading or ideas he is interested in at the time when it comes to planning his next projects or his exhibitions. Over the years, he has had 6 individual shows to date — the latest one being his 'The Shape of Water' series at Chapter II in Seoul, featuring intricately drawn close-ups of flowers that take up the whole canvas. According to Gim, "familiar things feel strange from time to time", and as he continues to put his inspirations on paper, his next endeavour will be one to watch.

Dukhoon Gim

The Hunting of the Snark
1051 mm x 748 mm

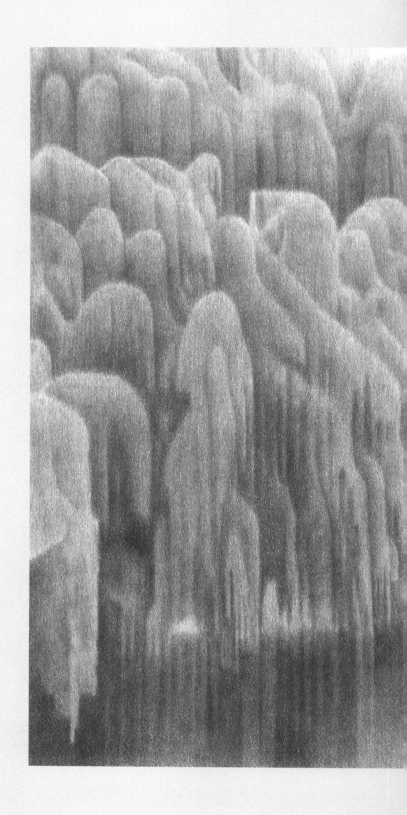

Dukhoon Gim

Where is Marion Crane
748 mm x 1051 mm

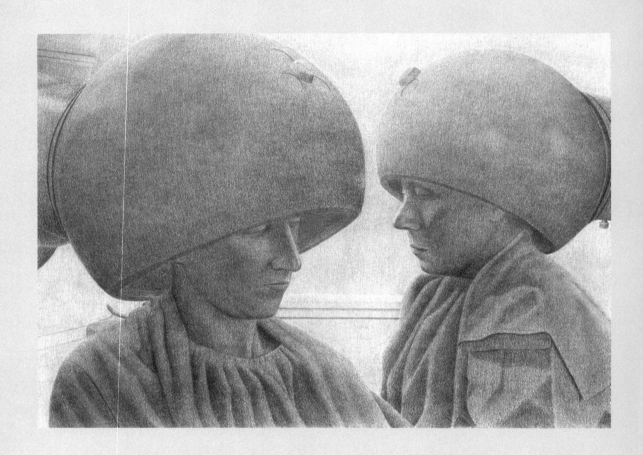

ARTIST TALK

Salon Time
525 mm x 748 mm

Dukhoon Gim

In Between
525 mm x 748 mm

ARTIST TALK

Cheese Burger
525 mm x 525 mm

Dukhoon Gim

Juniper
723 mm x 520 mm

Dukhoon Gim

Locomotive
1050 mm x 748 mm

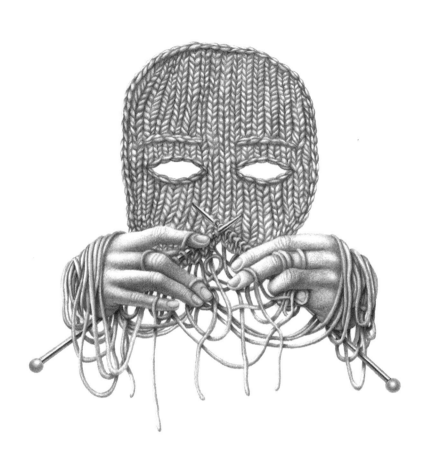

The Knitter
305 mm x 254 mm

ARMANDO VEVE

———

THE ENIGMATIC AND TRANSIENT WORLD OF ARMANDO VEVE

From intricate diagrams and cross-sections of organs and buildings to surreal collages of everyday objects, flora and fauna, Armando Veve's illustrated world is a compendium of strangely-fascinating scenarios that are refined to every detail.

Armando Veve is a Philadelphia-born and raised artist with an impressive portfolio of clients. With a focus on editorial illustrations, he has been commissioned by The New York Times, Wall Street Journal, The New Yorker and the like. The artist has also received accolades by American Illustration, Communication Arts, Spectrum, and the Society of Illustrators in NY. With his defined illustrative style and ambitious portfolio, Armando was named an ADC Young Gun by The One Club for Creativity and selected into the Forbes 30 under 30 list.

Armando undertook his artistic training in the Rhode Island School of Design, where he spent a semester in Rome for a European Honours Programme and graduated with honours in 2011. At that time, he enjoyed working with a very slow pen and ink technique, and would spend hours, days, and sometimes even months building soft stippled textures with the finest Rapidograph pens and custom-coloured inks. Armando especially loved how these drawings became records of thought created over long stretches of time. However as he began to approach editorial work, the artist realised that this time-consuming method was not sustainable, and he sought for a more forgiving medium that would allow for him to finish works at a faster pace.

While Armando's use of graphite grew out of necessity, he believed that it was predetermined that he would eventually switch to this medium as his pen began to lag behind his thoughts. "I think I would have slowly gravitated towards graphite even without the demand of the editorial work as I was feeling increasing tension between the slowness of the pen technique and the speed of my thinking," he recounts. "Graphite provided a more fluid connection between my brain and hand."

At the core of Armando's creative process is collage, a technique most prominent in many of his works. The 33 year old artist creates intricate collages of all things ordinary and strange, pulling different elements, thoughts, and images together that he collects constantly in notebooks

---

Armando Veve is an illustrator working in Philadelphia. His drawings have been recognised by American Illustration, Communication Arts, Spectrum, and the Society of Illustrators in NY. He was named an ADC Young Gun by The One Club for Creativity and selected into the Forbes 30 under 30 list.

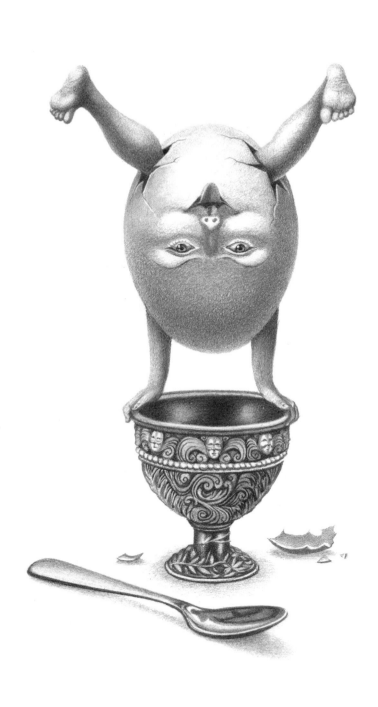

and his computer into a carefully-composed arrangement. "When I construct new compositions I collage these connective fragments to find unexpected relationships between disparate ideas," he explains. Some drawings have hidden metaphors and meanings waiting to be deciphered, like his editorial work for Smithsonian Magazine, Public Intellectuals, which depicts a shelf that displays the article's subjects in a series of imagery on a shelf. In the meantime, some are simply playful with a touch of comical surrealism, like the egg doing a headstand or the hound made of pasta in A Rake's Progress, a food-inspired drawing series for a restaurant in The Line Hotel DC.

The artist is constantly looking for inspiration — whether it is something he sees on a walk, or an image he encounters in a deep internet dive, or even his hometown of Philadelphia, which has proven to be a great source of inspiration for his work. "Finding connections between something old and new excites me. Some ideas I keep and integrate into my drawings, others I send to my sketch graveyard where they may one day be resurrected," Armando muses.

As seen in the various subjects and forms of his work, Armando has always drawn influence from anatomical and botanical diagrams, and had an affinity for the grotesque and absurd. Since he was young, the artist got most of his drawing inspiration from TV cartoons, children's books, Disney animated films, and comics. When he began studying illustration at the Rhode Island School of Design, he embraced the academic drawing style to articulate his ideas, and also did a lot of media and conceptual experimentation. It was not until after moving to Philadelphia in 2011 that Armando returned to a more technical drawing style through which he channels his humour and interest in the absurd. "As I get older, and especially after my dad's passing, I do find myself leaning more towards transient and enigmatic imagery that is more difficult to unpack," he adds.

His fascination with cartography, architectural models, toys, furniture design, and even the contraption-filled Rube Goldberg machines, result in their frequent appearances in his work. With an endless list of creative inspiration, Armando believes that he is most fascinated by imagery that abstracts and distils complex information in a way that is accessible.

Armando Veve

Egg Stand
305 mm x 254 mm,
Client: A Rake's Progress Restaurant

Armando Veve

The Hacienda Hedge
330 mm x 508 mm
Client: Bloomberg Markets

Like the exposed woodwork of the log in Motown Techno Ikebana, or the medical diagram-like style of Gene Therapy 2.0, Armando's work often inspires a deep sense of exploration between microscopic and macroscopic worlds. The artist loves to apply the language of these scientific illustrations to explore and expose the inner workings of all kinds of systems including the biological, the mechanical, and even the political.

"How can we take the chaos we live in, and organise it in a way that makes us think differently about our familiar environments?" He asks rhetorically.

With a portfolio filled with detailed collages of mesmerising dreamscapes and macabre imagery, one may wonder how these excruciatingly detailed works take form in Armando's mind. As an answer to this question, he tells us the two main approaches when creating his work. The majority of Armando's drawings begin with a thought or some kind of conceptual departure and a message to convey to the audience. However, like any artist working on commissions, the flow of his work also depends a lot on the deadline set by the client.

"Recently I have been enjoying drawing without too much foresight, and just allowing the process to unfold in a mysterious and organic way. However, if I am under a tight deadline I like to plan an idea before approaching the drawing," he says realistically. "It's a delicate balance of rehearsal and improvisation, and I think my most unexpected drawings always start as written thought."

Moreover, having been commissioned by big names such as National Geographic, Wired, and VICE to name a few, Armando also opens up on how he strikes a balance between sticking to the brief and keeping one's distinct voice while working on commercial projects.

To begin with, he tries not to distinguish his approach between personal and commercial projects, as he believes that all is rooted in the matter of problem-solving. The artist believes that the only difference with commercial work is that he is given a problem to solve, whereas in his personal work, he creates his own problems. With commercial projects, deadlines are a double-edged sword. While the deadlines commercial projects demand certainly help in finishing the work, being constantly

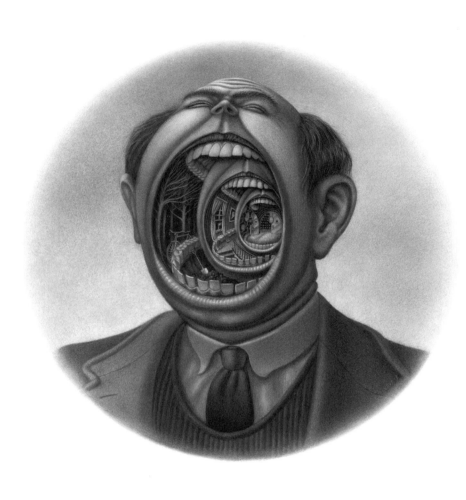

Armando Veve

The Third Policeman
622 mm x 622 mm,
Client: Hen's Teeth Prints

Armando Veve

ICON Poster
775 mm x 953 mm, Client: ICON The
Illustration Conference

265

Armando Veve

Public Intellectuais
333 mm x 402 mm
Client: Smithsonian Magazine

rushed in the creation process are not the most ideal way to produce art. However in reality, artists and creatives are often asked to finish work in a relatively fast timeline, and the pressure of an incessant time limit is definitely not healthy.

"I think this has only nourished, not hindered, my creative process since I have learned how to be intentional and efficient with my marks," he reveals, "Also, the wide range of topics I cover with my commercial work has introduced me to new subject matter and writing that has inspired my own independent projects, and I think it's healthy to maintain a combination of both."

Out of all the works that Armando has done in the past, he especially loved working on Cabinetarium, an illustrated deck of playing cards inspired by cabinets of curiosity, which he developed for Art of Play. The project took about a whopping two years to complete, but for Armando, it was truly a labour of love. "I had so much fun working with the team at Art of Play — Dan and Dave Buck and Adam Rubin. Seeing the work connect with audiences across the world has been exciting!"

While Armando's switch to graphite was partially motivated by its speed and immediacy, there is much to love about the simple medium. From delicate and ephemeral to loud and graphic, the humble lead pencil has a vast emotional range that allows the artist to channel themselves with different textures, shades, and strokes. "I often think about illustrating as writing with pictures, especially with graphite's associations with writing and ideation," he says.

"Although graphite is usually a starting point for my works, I'm always experimenting with other media and trying to widen my expressive range," explains Armando, "I'm amazed that I am still finding new ways of working with graphite even after 10 years of daily use."

There's no saying how many new stories Armando will tell in the future, but it goes without saying that they will all be wonderfully surreal and sublime at the same time.

Armando Veve

Cuckoo Clock
475 mm x 380 mm,
Client: A Rake's Progress Restaurant

Armando Veve

Escape Room
249 mm x 181 mm
Client: The New York Times Magazine

Acknowledgement

We would like to thank all the designers
and companies who were involved in
the production of this book. This project
would not have been accomplished
without their significant contribution
to its compilation. We would also like
to express our gratitude to all the
producers for their invaluable opinions
and assistance throughout this entire
project. Its successful completion owes
a great deal to many professionals in
the creative industry who have given us
precious insights and comments. And
to the many others whose names are
not credited but have made specific
input in this book, we thank you for your
continuous support the whole time.

Future Editions

If you wish to participate in viction:ary's
future projects and publications, please
send your website or portfolio to
we@victionary.com